All of This Was Once Under Water
poems

by Natalie Padilla Young

All of This Was Once Under Water
Text Copyright © 2023 by Natalie Padilla Young
Art Copyright © 2023 by Maximiliane Spieß

No part of this book may be used or reproduced without the permission of the publisher and copyright owner. However, small portions may be referenced for academic or review purposes.

Editor & Block Art: Chris Smith
Cover Art: Maximiliane Spieß

Fonts:
This book is set in various forms of Californian FB.

ISBN: 978-1-952730-11-5

Second Printing

Published by Quarter Press, LLC
Millen, GA
www.quarterpress.com

All of This Was Once Under Water
poems

by Natalie Padilla Young

Art by Maximiliane Spieß

Quarter Press
Millen, GA

A She and an Alien walk into a ~~bar~~, whoops, I mean, Utah. And so does Brigham Young. And there's a Monster, too, one that lives in the briny depths of the Great Salt Lake. This isn't a joke, though—this is Natalie Padilla Young's wonderfully inventive and dizzyingly spellbinding *All of This Was Once Under Water*. Laced with salt water and cryptozoology, these poems speak to the magic that is navigating landscapes, both familiar and foreign, with an alien as co-pilot. It's deeply weird, too, which is to say: it's wonderful.
    - Christina Olson, author of *The Anxiety Workbook*

All of This Was Once Under Water is entrancing, beguiling, disquieting —a collection of poetic dispatches from a terrain of lost faith and ecological decline. A genderless alien from another world, a philosophical monster residing in the Great Salt Lake, and a human "She" with a long-buried trauma: these are just some of the dramatis personae in this compendious collection that make the familiar strange again. Interspersed fragments of history about the birth of the Mormon Church comment ironically on our current state. The tone isn't elegiac. There is hope in these searching poems, in their sensuous encounter with nature—not to mention a love affair between alien and human. The wondrous attention, the wry melancholy, and the sly humor of these poems will allow readers to glimpse their own lives with new eyes.
    - Dan O'Brien, author of *Our Cancers*

Natalie Padilla Young's remarkable volume of poems, *All of This Was Once Under Water*, keenly limns the complex interstices of landscape, mystery, natural and human histories, and their cataclysmic interrelationships with environment, climate change, community, identity. Part geological exploration of the natural history of place, part settler colonialist history, part speculative space-age futurity, *All of This Was Once Under Water* is a testament to change, flux, and transformation. In crystalline, fleur de sel poems, Young deftly articulates a palimpsest of overlapping and competing belief systems. Who is alien, these poems ask? Who is monstrous? Here, science, spirituality, and apocrypha collide with the unknown, and fossil records attest to a natural history as seemingly unlikely as rumors of a prehistoric monster in the Great Salt Lake, or the arrival of aliens in Mormon country. As Young compellingly writes: "The monster is everything / She thinks She needs: a story / told, a reason to believe not to believe."

    ~ Lee Ann Roripaugh, author of
tsunami vs. the fukushima 50

*for Nano
my best editor, cheerleader, and partner*

Table of Contents

One

Prologue: The Cast ...

Sick with Rocky Mountain Spotted Fever, Brigham Young Looks Out Over the Salt Lake Valley for the First Time / 2

A Floridian Says, "I Could Never Live in a Place Like That" / 3

Capitol Reef / 5

Notes on Earth Life / 6

Too Many Humans End in a Crash / 7

Great White Sharks Must Move Forward to Breathe / 8

The Great Salt Lake—An Incomplete Timeline, Part V: Worker Sightings / 10

The Great Salt Lake has been shrinking since the rounding of the last ice age. / 11

The Flamingo on Shore—Pink Floyd, an Aviary Escapee / 13

The Great Salt Lake—An Incomplete Timeline, Part I: Infant Insects / 14

Alien and She Visit the North / 15

Discussing Earth Insects / 16

Alien Discovers a Sweet Tooth / 18

She's Diagnosing, Breaking Down the Day / 19

Two

71% of the Earth's Surface / 23

Attempt #2 to Spot the Monster / 24

The Great Salt Lake—An Incomplete Timeline, Part III: Pulled to Sea / 25

Fox Mulder and the Vampire Slayer / 26

Darwin Applied with a Garden Hose / 27

Stuck in a Watery Still / 28

An Ambush of Major and Minor—the Monster Sings / 29

The Great Salt Lake—An Incomplete Timeline, Part IV: Tourism for Generations / 32

HonK's $1 Store / 33

The Alien Collects a Pet / 34

From "Deseret" to "Utah" / 35

What She Misses About Being Mormon / 36

Of Course the Monster Had a Mother / 37
Sunday Dinners Are Awkward / 38
The Monster Stalks Seagulls / 39
Folklore from a combination of Mormon doctrine and settling new land leads to "Munchie" sightings on the Great Salt Lake / 40
"Kelpie" Sounds Nicer than "Monster" / 41
Pretending to be interviewed, the monster gets choked up, tells the cameraman to shut the damn thing off. / 42
The Alien Takes the Human's Tears / 44
Much of the Universe's / 46

Three

Exhausted by more than just tears and empty ice cube trays, the human addresses the alien's water experiments. / 51
The Monster Laughs at the Accounts / 52
Earth Ghosts / 53
Utah Complications / 54
For Classification Purposes / 56
Sorting Bulk / 57
The Mums Are Always Dying / 58
Sacrament Meeting Started the Three Hours of Church on Sunday / 59
This Rainbow / 60
The Great Salt Lake—An Incomplete Timeline, Part II: A Monster and Salt Water Farming / 62
Fish, Bigotry and Self-defense or The Alien Reconsiders Earth Hobbies / 63
The Monster Reveals the Grave Robber's Fate / 64

Four

The Smog that Rides the Salt Lake/Davis County Line / 69
The Great Salt Lake—An Incomplete Timeline, Part VII: Demolished Fences, Cars and Trees / 70
Victim: / 71
Discussing Customs / 72
The Trouble with Clothing / 73
Via friction and gravity, a black hole is marked not by absence, but by its interaction with what surrounds it / 74

The monster looks into the dark heavens and considers how things would be different if he believed in a higher power. / 75
Jealousy and Greed Are Green or The Alien Tries to Explain his Flat Temper / 76
The Great Salt Lake—An Incomplete Timeline, Part VI: Disappearances / 77
The Monster Sees Calves and Feet Off the North Shore / 79
The Alien Chose He, but Now Wants to Be a She / 80
The Elusive Equation's Solution / 82
What the Alien Thinks to Say to She / 83
Tantrum / 84
She Writes Notes to the Pagoda Tree, Ties Them to the Branches One by One / 85
Here Is What's Left of Lake Bonneville / 86

Notes and Sources / 89
Acknowledgments / 91

One

Let's have a disaster, a lake made of salt, a blackout. Everything riots and unspools, the whole room on one side and all the sound winking out.

—from "Exuberance," Hillary Gravendyk

But verily I say unto you, I have decreed that your brethren which have been scattered shall return to the lands of their inheritances, and shall build up the waste places of Zion.

Doctrine and Covenants 103:11
(Mormon Book of Scripture)

Prologue: The Cast

She: A human woman. A little pieced. A little glued. Like a Boy Scout, She carries belief and a pocket-knife at all times, for paring, to learn utility and strokes.

Earth: Also a little broken. Aliens walk about as immgrants. Green cards no longer relevant.

Aliens: Want to fit in. Do not camouflage themselves (minus fashion and gender). They expected information, a movie trailer—not handheld galactics or the need for a cleanup crew.

Utah: What Earth is cropped down to for the story's sake. Alien in its own right.

Great Salt Lake: Vestige of the ancient sea, a body will float without effort. Its body continues to shrink, not without explanation. An unidentified monster.

The Monster: Lockness. Dinosaur. A salt creature who sings, cares more and less about the antelope on his islands. Has never swallowed a mouthful of fresh water.

Sick with Rocky Mountain Spotted Fever, Brigham Young Looks Out Over the Salt Lake Valley for the First Time

Propped up, blank desert
below. *It is enough. This
is the place, drive on.*

These words moved along
the wagon trail, a journey
ending for a start

in a land without
persecution, a vast slate
ready to perfect

A Floridian Says,
"I Could Never Live in a Place Like That."

A few creeks scattered about,
the sound of rounded pebbles and mallards
behind gates.
A set of sprinklers, the bathroom faucet—
the only ways to wet July knuckles.

An instant after Brigham Young decreed
in high fever, *This is the right place*,
a number of his saints said,
No.
Spun their wagon wheels and blistered heels
against cracks in the dirt
to return East or urge their oxen forward
to promises of something gold,
something moist.

This place is a high-mountain desert.
A desert.

The aliens don't care
how many pollens itch the throat
or if you see Begonias that thrive—
those things stay alive
because someone hoses them down
every day.

Every day
someone
hoses them down.

Capitol Reef

Now miles from any real city, roaming
in a red rock bowl. She recalls a time
at 13 when a stray attacked.

Walking the sea floor, boots fill
with red dust: rusty animal
heads, pioneers' tombstones.

Commitment not an option. No way
for her to describe, to know how.
Still, its giant departure is clear, a pulse
outlined in chalk.

She claims old bites
are good reason to give up
an adopted dog after six days.

The look in the canine eyes:
endless. The stare—
like finding a giraffe
body under a skiff of snow.

Breaking things
off, keeping things up.

All of this was once under water.

Notes on Earth Life

A child in a pink coat leaves her music lesson. Her cheeks match her coat. Her father sells insurance based on how long an equation expects a person to stay alive.

The old man died. Sometimes humans just die. And you cannot save them. Sometimes humans do not die, and you cannot save them.

There is a television program about a real human family doing normal Earth things—there are many programs with real people doing what people always do. Humans stop doing what they do to watch.

When humans determine an animal is too ill, they end the life. This is called "putting it to sleep." It costs $66.87 (US) for a 20-lb. dog to sleep.

The capitol city sits in a valley between mountains, trapping air. Weather reports call a day with dirty air "hazy." The haze hurts to breathe. The haze is measured in particles and colors.

The adult male across the street can play the piano and make sculptures. He plays well. This is a stimulation for many females, particularly those who enjoy show tunes.

Being tall with tight skin, that is what humans like.
What do humans and our kind like? Water. Blankets. Sugar.
These things are both new and old to us.

Too Many Humans End in a Crash

She chooses aliens,
medium to small ones with wild eyes, slick olive
skin, the inside of their mouths: pimentos.

They're a lot like what you thought,
but not all. Moist, they prefer humidity. Some settled here
in the high desert anyway, missions or a need

for work. The spots along their limbs so light
they mingle like wet ink, a slow gradient. Forest deep,
alligators, salamanders. Neither male nor female,

they are not kind, a tad ruthless
about flags and radio signals. At least they're honest.
She knows what she's going to get. At first

it's hard to forgive the way their landings took
pieces from her—fields and heat. Most structures
survived, so interactions become—not betrayal—

compromise. She likes the aliens' lack
of hair, the smooth scalps, smooth everywhere. Most choose
a sex, less complications to pick, blend in with trousers

or pumps, paint their lips and wear hats. It's not easy
to walk on Earth looking like a movie.

Great White Sharks Must Move Forward to Breathe

She's to the point where every highway garbage bag
or blown-out tire is an animal

to mourn. The scenes are a trick of the eye,
a catch and jump of her chest

landing heavy. Line of sight moves
back and forth between *true* and *history*.

*

500 remain off the South African coast,

3,500 total. Making the great white more endangered
than the tiger.   She's never seen one

gliding behind glass, because no aquarium can keep one.
No longer able to reach 15 mph

without space and something to chase, the creature passes
again and again   away. Sometimes reaching 20 feet

of despair and relief. She is landlocked and can do
nothing for the shark. Nothing for the flattened animals

on the roads around her house—too many
to be a mistake,   mistaken,

an accident.

*

All of those facts
merely best guesses from the best available angle

at a certain moment. The fiction
of grief doesn't settle her stomach, knowing

an actual dead body lies somewhere, in final display
of perfect timing.

*

What if it's the teenage boy next door
who will grow up and regret it? What if

it's not or he won't?   Sometimes the act of watering
the potted plants seems impossible, excess

shed to concrete.   What if the concentration
should be on the little dog   who stops at every puddle
for a drink?

The Great Salt Lake—An Incomplete Timeline, Part V: Worker Sightings

1877:   At dusk of early summer
several Barnes & Co. Salt Works employees reported
a huge crocodile body and horse head.

The creature made a fearsome bellow and charged
the workers, who promptly ran

up a nearby hill and hid
in the bush until morning. Some believe it
was a buffalo.

The Great Salt Lake has been shrinking since the rounding of the last ice age.

The monster has lasted centuries
        with little light, in one place.

This lake once spanned hundreds of monsters,
        millions of gallons to roam.

Now he has a small city, a village
        deep enough to safely travel. He doesn't mind much,
but wonders about humans and sun.

What will be done when the many things collected
        are uncovered? Bones and rings and rocks.

What was lost. Cast off.
        The trash of time. He and his house release
only what breathes oxygen or is little enough

to evaporate.
        Life gets smaller. Salt gets thicker.

The monster doesn't consider lost love or favorites,
        the monster wants to know

the view from that hilltop, what fresh water tastes like,
        how big a lung feels
when it inhales.

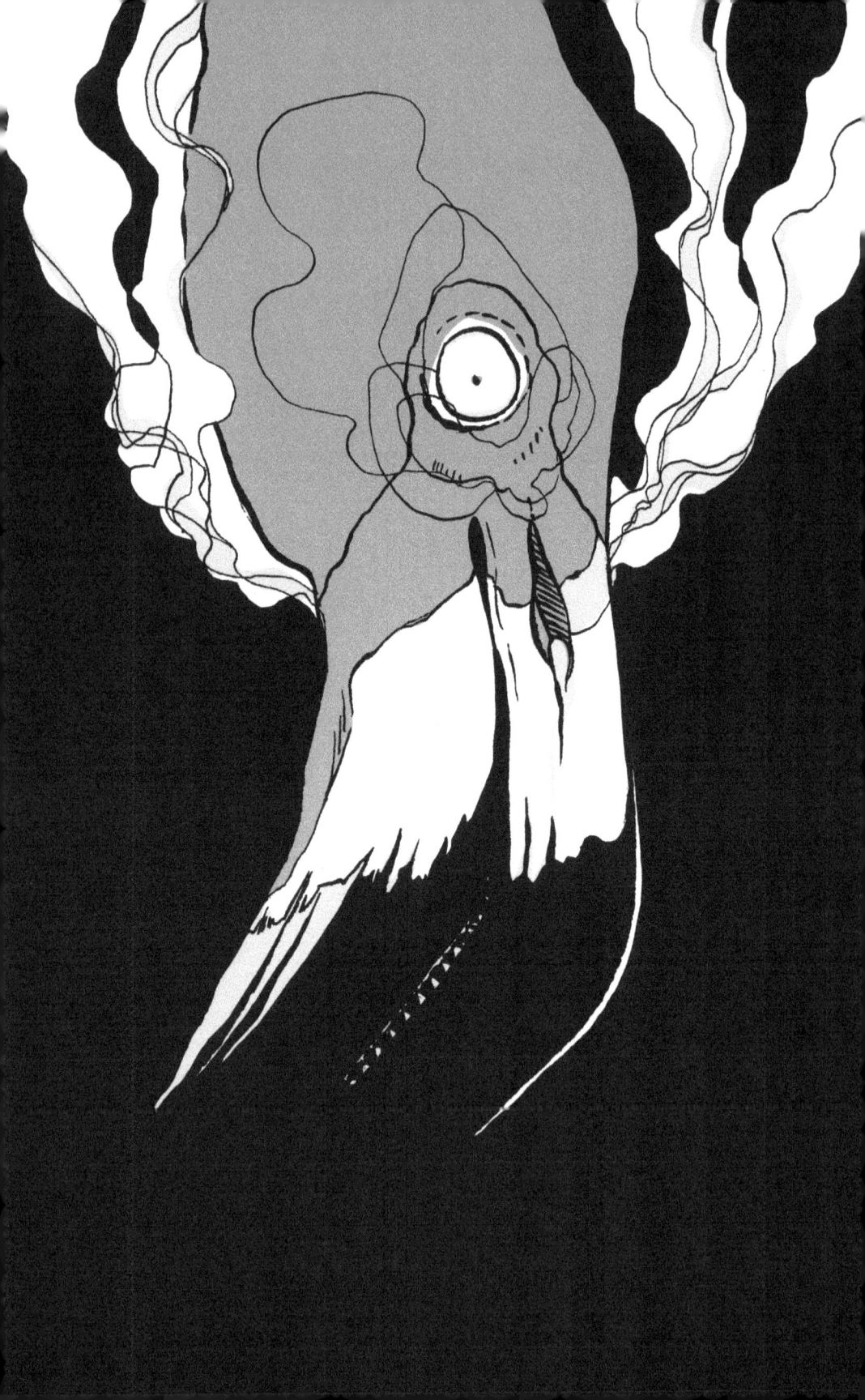

The Flamingo on Shore—Pink Floyd, an Aviary Escapee

through the water
the monster catches
from the corner of his eye
a tall pink bird

seasonal
alone at the lake
like the monster

but chooses
when to fly away
and when to stay

the monster stares
for hours:

lanky legs
thin gray stems
fluorescent knees
one at a time
holding the bright body

while it sleeps
while it filters brine shrimp
through salt water

more pink
with each feeding

sometimes it's the most
color he's seen

sometimes it's the only
color he sees.

The Great Salt Lake—An Incomplete Timeline, Part I: Infant Insects

1843-44: Along the shores, John C. Fremont found
accumulations of brine fly larvae
20 feet wide, one-foot deep—a wading pool worth.

Alien and She Visit the North

This and an egg timer brought them together. The highly sensitive and hardboiled can be magnetic late in a long day, dressed in cologne, fluorescents—an alien favorite. Something to do with rod-to-cone distribution, a balancing act in our planet's atmosphere.

Things carry and fall in the small northern valley of cheese. The alien and She go fishing in the reservoir. Dangle lines without color. She reels it in, looks it in the eye and releases. Each one a little too familiar.

He keeps them all. Slurps them down raw. Doesn't bother to explain the taste. Small chunks of Velveta litter the tackle box. She asks if he wonders. He says he doesn't need to. Says his kind can't go near the Great Salt Lake, forbidden by unwritten rule to locate the monster of a land-locked sea. Sunk, spurred, she must see the one-and-only in her own backyard.

Discussing Earth Insects

A praying mantis perches on the coffee shop doorframe,
the alien is intrigued. He takes out the human's camera.

Look at how sturdy its skin is,
how mean. Like it will reach out and slice
anything that gets too close.

He wants to know where insects come from.
Where the aliens come from insects don't really exist.
He wants to know,
                  What is the difference
between a moth and a butterfly?

She doesn't know the science
behind classification, the pieces and parts,
something about antennae—smooth club vs. pipe cleaner,
fuzzy vs. shaved.

           They are not small birds?
No. No bones.

She explains how she sees,
                A moth can't resist light.

The alien considers the distinction.
So, I am the butterfly   *and you are the moth.*

Alien Discovers a Sweet Tooth

Anxious for the next encounter
he sends signals
special condiments
more signals more sweet
more pitted fruit

He's right
given the time and spices
the human can talk herself out of
or into anything

She's Diagnosing, Breaking Down the Day

Forget today's dirty haze, think of the clouds acting

distant like a geisha's white foundation—thin, even, trained
for years in the art before becoming official—officially looking down

at armadillos, armor-plated creatures on the road linked
to leprosy, and then, instantly, to Jesus and curing,

instant miracles. His followers following all those years and seconds
ago, before the metaphors got complicated: Sheep always faithful,

but never brave, run alongside while also running away
to safety. The same kind of safe

human bodies try to build with fruits and spices. Orange,
the intense color of turmeric works

through blood, eases what's inflamed—protection
in powder and a full moon overhead, full of that honest,

round face. And honestly, She's never been able to see
the man up there. Features visible with a squint and far reach of what

She does see: gray spots, shadow and stillness. Still, She cannot tell
where the clouds end and the haze begins.

Two

*And while we wonder at the number of angels that might fit
on the end of a stinger, at a heaven that might follow*

heaven ...

   —from "The Stitches that Hold the World Together," Mark Wagenaar

*The desert shall rejoice, and blossom as the rose ...
And the parched ground shall become a pool ...
And a highway shall be there, and a way ...*
Isaiah 35: 1, 7, 8

71% of the Earth's Surface

Immersed, objects are closer—new—
when wet. The alien examines. A wad of gum
                         sinks into a fountain, liquid mass

            slowing gravity.

With the right conditions
water will take on any shape: sculptures and cubes
         pools   steam and falls.

He travels to see what he can—from big bodies to ponds—practices
skipping stones
               until flick and release   the rock walking on water
is second nature.

At home, he fills different containers
          ¾ to the top, ½ empty, ¼ left—

               drops various items, studies
blankets and waves and force   fold in   explode out.

A butter knife taps   each glass a different note
each note   contained movement.

     Small stars of air appear as water sits, pop
as the cup tips.

The alien brings multiple kettles to a boil. Whistles sound off

       until the liquid is gone,

bubbled past high

        specific heat.   A kitchen full of clouds
and smoke.

Attempt #2 to Spot the Monster

Scuba gear in the bed of the truck. The same kind
her father used to scoop out tropical fish for their tank,

from a different body of water, before sunset colors
defined air quality and foreign threats.

This dive is not for swimming rainbows,
this is to prove a creature neither man nor fish,

lives in the Great Salt Lake. And the creature is happy
to be ignored, happy to have humans worry

about energy and fires, about roasting hot dogs.
The marshmallow smoke a signal to the universe.

The edges are bubbling and She's watching, eyeing
each one for reflection. A pupil. His teeth. A tail.

The Great Salt Lake—An Incomplete Timeline, Part III: Pulled to Sea

1870:   Whirlpools open subterranean channels,
           thought to drain into the Pacific
           Ocean. One man said

           his schooner was almost drawn in.

           Water spouts—tornadoes over water—
           the more likely source.

Fox Mulder and the Vampire Slayer

She knows the other life, the truth
Mulder always knew
was out there. As far as She can tell

vampires are absent, but there is the hope
they exist, and of course, She looks
for the monster in the salt lake
more than is healthy.

What would be helpful to tell Buffy
(you know, the Vampire Slayer)
about her obsession?
It's not a calling. You hunt

*because something happened
at age eight. Something that should be
worked through—
slow—a session a week.*

Agent Mulder should try, too,
though he may be beyond repair. Wishing
he were here to see
the aliens living on Earth,

She dyes her hair
red, tattoos her inner arm: *I want
to believe.*

Darwin Applied with a Garden Hose

Hand watering a corner of lawn, again—a sad replication
of nature that's anything
but natural

in such dry landscape. 50 days without rain—nearly
the opposite of Noah and the ark.
A moth flutters

out of grass, makes its entrance into the enormous,
cobalt night. And for the first time She worries, or perhaps
just wonders,

what happens to these furry nymphs with the onset of an actual storm.
Imagines wings sogged in droplets, antennae hung over
large brown eyes;

earth filled with quick-moving moisture, pounding thunder and still
wings thinner than paper flap on. It's a question
of survival

and She, a barefoot woman with a garden hose, deems it a miracle in this
open air littered with insects and theories—
theory's insects.

Stuck in a Watery Still

She sees the monster
as an illustration

sketched in charcoal with wide strokes
defining body, lightly shaded parentheses

of movement, water in grayscale—not flesh and bone
and tail—like imagining a centaur

or being a pioneer. Standing at the edge
of any body of water, She returns to him,

lets the water swim over her toes, pretends
the sting of gnats are a swipe from the ends

of limbs lifting above the surface—pelts of water
ping the skin. Proud

of the welts, the miniature kisses
dotting her cheeks, She kneels and washes

faces in salt water. The monster is everything
She thinks She needs: a story

told, a reason to believe not to believe.

An Ambush of Major and Minor—
the Monster Sings

An underwater witness,
he felt the wagons and handcarts,

the Mormons rumbling
the valley, and knew everything

about their new ground, knew
the square inches riddled with salt
had once been his living room. He felt
the building,

the thunks and thuds
of lean-tos and pews, the swift start
of empire. He heard generations
and prayers

being made. Heard
their songs—the combined power,
hundreds of voices singing *Zion*—one giant,
desperate beauty.

**

Over a hundred years and still
the notes linger
just below the surface, knock
his chest in sleep, tumble
from his mouth
as he swims. Pains of faith and cheer

on repeat. These songs
he sings

to a thrumming, a glug. To an end.

The Great Salt Lake—An Incomplete Timeline, Part IV: Tourism for Generations

1875:   James Wickham supposedly released two whales
into the lake as a tourist attraction.

A few sightings, then disappearance.

1890:   A pod of whales spotted swimming, possible
offspring from 15 years earlier. It is doubtful

marine mammals could live in such
extreme salinity.

HonK's $1 Store

Aisle 2B: shelf upon shelf
of pastel porcelain animals. Lavender
hippos with polka-dots and a slight

peach-like fuzz. A kitten in a sweater
that spells L U V E
in fake stitches. Two pink

puppies play patty cake. She picks up one
with a droopy left eye,
drop of red lacquer nuzzled in

the tear duct, an extra lump
of porcelain on the out-stretched paw
scratches her pinkie. Returned to the shelf,

the game resumes. She mustn't
take the puppy home; could never
stop running her fingers over

the one-dollar defects.

The Alien Collects a Pet

The alien decides to get a dog—
a big one.

The human's never had a long-term pet
so She's skeptical,

These things are very expensive.

> I created a budget. We'll take him
> on walks. He'll bark at strangers,
> keep burglars away.

She begins to talk about raking leaves,
bagging the leaves, eating salmon and rice.

> *Do you want to know his name?*

I read it on the tag: Charles.

She knew a Charles back in math class.
His shoulders were too small.

The alien grabs the leash.
She recites more chores. Garbage.
Dishes.

> He needs to go out. Do you want to come?
> We can take the trash too.

Listen. Here's the thing:
I've never been good
at sharing.

From "Deseret" to "Utah"

Utah became a state in 1896, nearly half a decade after the first attempt.

The name change was one
of the lesser trades to get
statehood, the biggest

being surrender—
the ban of polygamy—
marriage for union.

What She Misses About Being Mormon

It's taken awhile
to get to this point

where the alien knows enough
to ask questions

where She is able
to answer

from a sturdy place.

What does She miss
about going

each week? Support,
community.

The ritual.

A holy gesture
a meditation

in congregation
blessed bits of bread, shots

of water and comfort
knowing you know.

But knowing She's done
it's the hymns

She misses
most: too sad,

too happy, too slow.
Everything precious

in song,
in long and short,

in sweeping release.

Of Course the Monster Had a Mother

when the water was choppy   all

               the two could do was
rock   back and forth

              she would sing
notes low
              enough to
              make a body tremble

              make schools of fish scatter

shards

              bits   she

              led him down deeper
where storms quiet

              in dark

long   long   ago   seems
short
              small

and still   her moving

comfort is a cradle

through this
              solitude
              extended

life

Sunday Dinners Are Awkward

The alien makes her parents uneasy.
For them, recent past resonates   in minor key—

the tension   of the aliens' arrival: hostility
over crops and water,   destruction
from landing.

They don't know what   to say
to him. Small talk runs dry quickly and She strains
to make connections,   rummages
through sports and weather, but the similarities
are short.

Her parents don't understand how to live
with the ambiguity—   how
it works—   not male, not female.   Questions
often appear offensive.

This week it's a whole chicken. Dad slices and circles
the plate in perfect pattern. The alien passes
on the bird,

    No, thank you,   followed by family silence.
    I'm sure your chicken is delicious.
    If I ate meat...

Dad rolls his eyes. Mom pats Dad's hand.

You eat fish—that's meat.

    To us, it's different.

Just fish, huh?   *No wonder you all smell.*

The Monster Stalks Seagulls

He waits for the daring ones
willing to perch beyond the shore,
the greedy ones
who don't want to share.

He eats a bird whole,
sometimes several a day.
There's a lot to sustain and not much
can live in this water.

The monster studies
their flight, the somewhat short wingspan,
songs nothing like his own.
Does boldness

make the bird
taste different? A savor
not from salt, a gamey season
of adrenaline. Certain sadness

dangling on the echo, the lingering note
swallowed.

Folklore from a combination of Mormon doctrine and settling new land leads to "Munchie" sightings on the Great Salt Lake.

Giant, white Indians
on the major islands, alive
riding elephants

live elephants on
the islands, an Indian tribe
swathed in pure white skin

"Kelpie" Sounds Nicer than "Monster"

The monster's been around long enough; he could be one
        of those tales spun, evolved lake legend—

a shape-shifting water spirit appearing as a horse or walking
        on land as a human with hooves. A kelpie

was warning to keep away from the water
        and handsome strangers.

A kelpie abducted and devoured victims then left
        entrails at the water's edge. The monster contemplates this

        over-the-top act and decides he might
trade an ability to tread on dry ground

for the violence required. A human would be a more satisfying meal
        than a seagull. He mouths the word

into his salty reflection: *Kelpie, Kelpie,* K E L P I E E

Something is off—the letters feel too nice
        in his mouth. Too sterile. Despite the vulgar stories

the kelpie had a bridle and if stolen, became imbued
        with magic. The last thing the monster wants

        is humans coming after him for more
than a good look. The monster pushes the sweet-sounding word

through his teeth one more time and decides to simply be
        a monster.

Pretending to be interviewed, the monster gets choked up, tells the cameraman to shut the damn thing off.

Your environment doesn't change
much from day to day, you see
the same things. What inspires you?

>I spend time remembering, wondering
>what birds see
>when they fly away.

Does that help generate new ideas?

>I don't have much use for such things.

You don't wear clothing. How does that feel?

>I guess you're looking for "liberating,"
>But how would I know?

It's so quiet out here.

>The quiet came gradually,
>not a sudden silence.

Is it peaceful?

>It's not peaceful—
>it's not disturbing.
>
>If everything was brought back
>at once...the noise, the movement
>
>I miss,
>but could I still handle it?

*You lived through a lot—more than most books
can claim. What keeps you
going? What's next?*

>I'd like to be surrounded by something
other than salt water; to step on dry ground;
someone to look and call
me lovely.

The Alien Takes the Human's Tears

places them under a microscope
to reveal primal language

dehydrated and inspected, the salt formation
a suspect
of circumstance:

Grief crystallizes in empty streets, the dismantled
brick walls
of a looted city.

Onions plant a fern quilt in a snowflake
sheet. Geometry's
hard edges and blocks burst

from drips of laughter. Ice, metal
work and coral collide to build a blue print
encompassed

by crowds dispersing
in the uncertainty of change. And with a blink
a slide of the lid

waters
a cutaway of earth, roots reaching
beyond human

experience
like a drop of the ocean.

after "Topography of Tears," a photo series by Rose-Lynn Fisher

Much of the Universe's

water is produced
as a byproduct of star
formation. Newborn

pushing its way out-
ward from gas and dust. A fuse
to meld a rain storm.

Three

They told us our gods would outlive us, but they lied.

—from "Distant Sky," Nick Cave & The Bad Seeds

There are three things that are never satisfied, yea, four things that say not, It is enough:

The grave; and the barren womb; the earth that is not filled with water; and the fire that saith not, It is enough.

Proverbs 30:15–16

Exhausted by more than just tears and empty ice cube trays, the human addresses the alien's water experiments.

Did you know the ocean's pH
is nearly identical to human blood?

        Which feels true,
        though it's probably a myth.

What does every piece of life
come down to?

Two hydrogen atoms
clinging
to an oxygen.

        That's a lot of pressure
        for three molecules.

Fascination is understandable
even obsession.

    And yet
no matter the small hinge
this all rests on

you can't alter chemistry—
the way water never changes

its constant
change.

The Monster Laughs at the Accounts

burnt red eyes
looked straight at us
bubbling water like a boiling pot

a giant manatee
a beaver, dinosaur-big
no pupils, no one's seen before

humps four times the size of
gaping mouth
dolphin slick

just a fallen tree, a floating log
wide as a pool, thin as
a pole, 20 meters from head to

knocked our oars away
spotted, striped, *chills ran down*
snake torso, eel body

smell of sulfur
scent of lavender, *swam under and out of*
a bass-line hum

rotting fish
breath
the footage shaky, pixelated

reptile, Satan mammal
overexposed
devil

who rules these waters

Earth Ghosts

The light is morning: a slow spread with most of the landscape long and lean in shadow. The front yard is an orchard: fruit fallen and fruit on the branch give a crowded smell to the half-lit air. The alien startles from movement between leaves, cloaked by trees and said shadow: a white horse softly chews the fallen apples. So soft it's hard to believe he exists. Half a mile up the hill: a flat open field without structure or crop whose purpose seems to be to wait for a purpose. Two weeks ago this waiting field bobbed with prairie dogs, their small heads popping in and out click, click, clicking, *Danger!* at the alien's approach. Now the ground is silent, littered with soda bottles and doors to empty tunnels. The alien looked into these creatures: due to dwindling wide, open spaces, prairie dogs are protected, listed *Endangered*. Which means: the field was emptied by the Forest Service rules and relocation cages. Or: someone else came with no rules, no cages and a label of *Pest*. Puffed like half a balloon, a white bag rolls at the edge of the lot, over one dirt mound and then another.

Utah Complications

1.   Attempting to Explain State History to the Alien

... the white gulls upon the black crickets, like hosts of heaven and hell contending,
until the pests were vanquished and the people were saved.
—Orson F. Whitney, Mormon Settler and Apostle

A piece of the truth lies
in the bird's real name: *California gull.*

Early settlers almost starved because of a cricket
invasion, insects as big as a man's thumb.

Divine intervention (or migration)
brought flocks of gulls

who filled the air with white wings and cries,
settled on the fields, feasted and became

Utah's state bird. Oral history is muddled—
Sunday school taught her and She tells the alien

how seagulls saved the pioneers'
crops from grasshoppers. Google clarifies

and confuses with more truth, claiming
the *Mormon cricket* was likely a *shieldback katydid,*

changing color in mob situations, swarming
fields in a cloak of black.

Whatever the true labels, the bugs came and ate
corn and wheat, squashes and melon.

And no matter if they came for God
or the salt lakes, legions of birds

gorged themselves and saved a people's
right to name a miracle.

2.   After Studying State History, the Alien Kills Weeds

Persecution is not uncommon in this state
or its people: Mormons, polygamists.

Massacres less common: Mountain Meadows;
Bear River Shoshone.

And though the alien has second thoughts
about extermination, he's started

spraying unstoppable weeds
in the yard. The poison streams

out, accidentally hitting
an adult grasshopper here, a baby there.

Camouflaged so perfectly
it's always too late to retreat.

The alien takes concern
to the neighbor in a large sunhat.   *Don't worry*

> *they're pests   they'll take*
> *your garden   your greens   your sage*
> *munch and   pock*
>   *they're asking for it.*

The sun is directly overhead and he can hear
a cricket chirping.

Is the insect in trouble or confused
about what is appropriate,

what we do and do not do in the daylight?

For Classification Purposes

What about the plants in the backyard who nest, still clothed, behind a fence? These plants are more like weeds.   A brood parasite, the cowbird lays eggs in nests of other small perchers, tosses in with the humming, the raptors.   She never thought to tell the difference between tulip and daffodil stamen. But there they are, stripped in the flowerbed, no mistaking who is who.   Isn't it strange that birds and crocodiles are the only living descendants of dinosaurs, that birds have their very own class, not mammal, not insect, not reptile?   (Raptors make her think twice.)   And the weeds in total? More like jungle aiding, abetting a grasshopper herd.   A weed by her feet, normally short and squat, mimics another: elongated stem, thinned leaves.   Every few pretend, camouflage into the flock.   Brown-headed babies sneak room and board at someone else's expense, a shortage of space and food to go around. Pulling away the jungle.   Scientists categorize birds and reptiles mainly on the basis of their ankles.   Look at these two dandelions. Would you guess the seeds are the same?   Real parents relieved from investment and building, risk of loss to hungry burglars (raccoons, cats, meat lovers) lowered.   The seeds' specialty is spreading, hatching only as conditions prove correct.   None caring to hide.   When She said "pulling," it's more—it's plucking, it's eradication.   The taxonomy is complicated: *common, fleshy, horned, wandering.*   The nomenclature not fully resolved.

Sorting Bulk

Buying blueberries and spinach at the warehouse
where all that's sold is bulk
means commitment.

For a household of two it's at least a week
of daily blues and greens: whole,
chopped, boil, blend.

On day six, the berries come out of the fridge,
She plucks through, removes the rot, stores
the less sad in a plastic bag.

A miniature caterpillar crawls on the counter,
before She thinks:
smash.

Thumb to speck. His guts a patch of midnight
blue inking a fingerprint.
Evidence

of his commitment.

The Mums Are Always Dying

> *We're gonna do it easy, but then we're gonna do the finish rough.*
> —Tina Turner's intro to "Proud Mary"

Holding out a bundle of mums
from the grocery store
to offset a bad day,

She tells the alien how hard it is
to remember everything, every day to do
every thing, how proud she feels

to have shopped and gathered
so much, saved
dollars with coupons and sales.

> *Why bother with it all?*
> *I can fix your trouble. I know how*
> *to make a run for it. Metal cart flying*
>
> *out automatic doors—we could get far*
> *away—take off and live without*
> *the ground.*

Days later, the petals start to wilt, giant puffs
in a droop. She decides and says
Tina Turner's head looks like an aging mum.

> *My kind, your kind... we all look*
> *like one dying flower*
> *or another.*

Sacrament Meeting Started the Three Hours of Church on Sunday

A friend taught her how to pass the time: flip through
the hymn book and add "in the bathtub"
after any song title: "How Great Thou Art...in the Bathtub"
"Now Let Us Rejoice...in the Bathtub"

"Did You Think to Pray in the Bathtub?" "Know This,
That Every Soul Is Free in the Bathtub."
An hour of speeches broken up by hymns,
prayers and eating Christ's blood and body (blessed,

white Wonder Bread and a doll's cup
of water for each worthy member).
She no longer sits through church meetings or questions
her questioning, though often hums those hymns

around the house, slips holy
ingrained choruses into a tub of hot water.
Ears immersed, She can hear the sounds
of her own choir. The heart's *bahdum, bah-dum*

bahdum, too fast for its own good. "Rejoice a Glorious Sound
Is Heard...in the Bathtub." Rustling
empty stomach, gurgle escalates
to a shout. Whooshes of breath tunnel in and out. Hard enough

to simply sit still, then left to a porcelain amphitheater—
"Where Can I Turn for Peace?" In the bathtub
thuds whirl. "Come Along, Come Along"
"With All the Power of Heart and Tongue."

Maintenance of this submerged body
too tough, too much "Master the Tempest Is Raging."
Not enough still, small whisper:
"Ye Simple Souls Who Stray"

"Let Us All Press On."

This Rainbow

Written
or painted, shot or sung.

It has already.
But She can't help
this rainbow: strong

at both ends,
every color equally
present.

Pales
in the camera lens, invisible
out loud

and here. She will never see
Noah, each animal pair
march

through the just right
arch. The thick
part. This rainbow

followed
for 200 miles.

And everything made
better, for something

stunning
for such length.
Not even poor

drivers or roadside
animals
could make the rainbow stop.

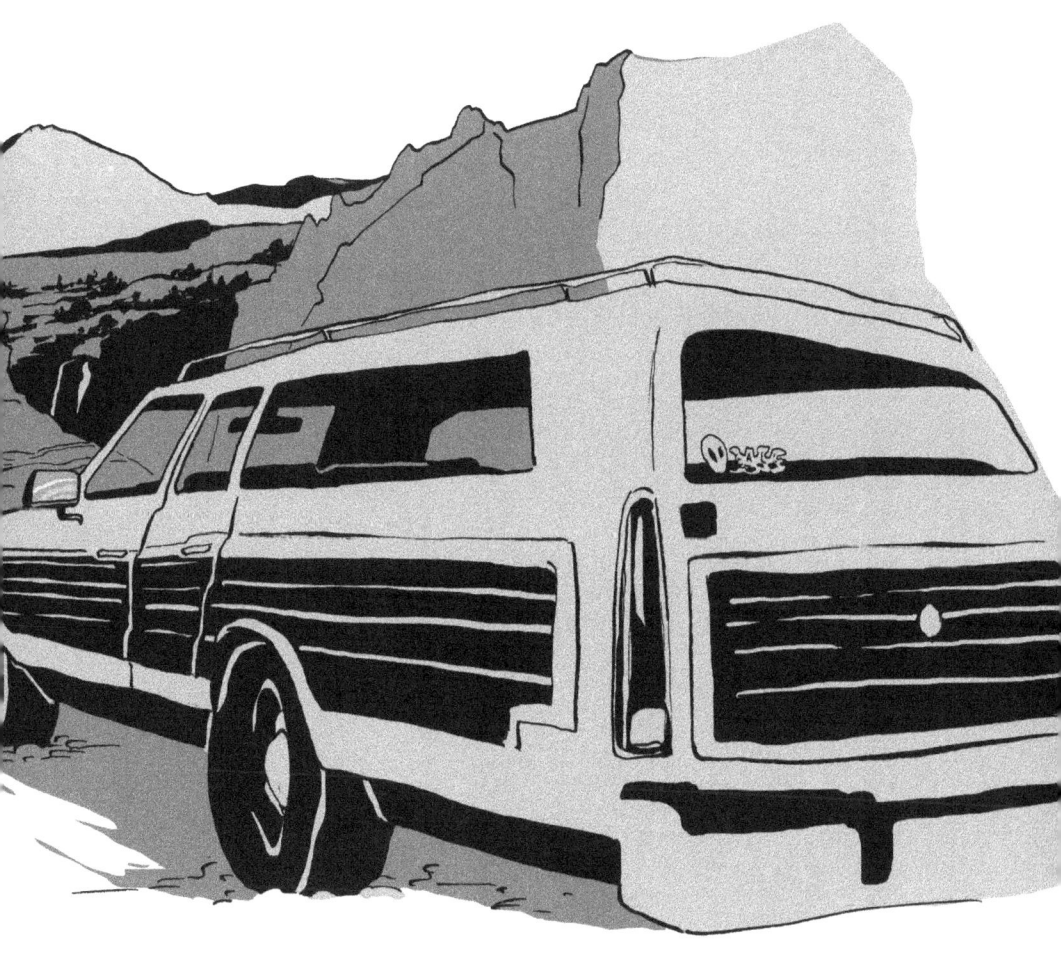

The Great Salt Lake—An Incomplete Timeline, Part II: A Monster and Salt Water Farming

1847:   A certain Brother Bainbridge reported a monster with a dolphin-like body.

1853:   An editorial advocates placing sea life in the lake as potential food sources.

Oysters, eels, fish and crabs planted—none survived.

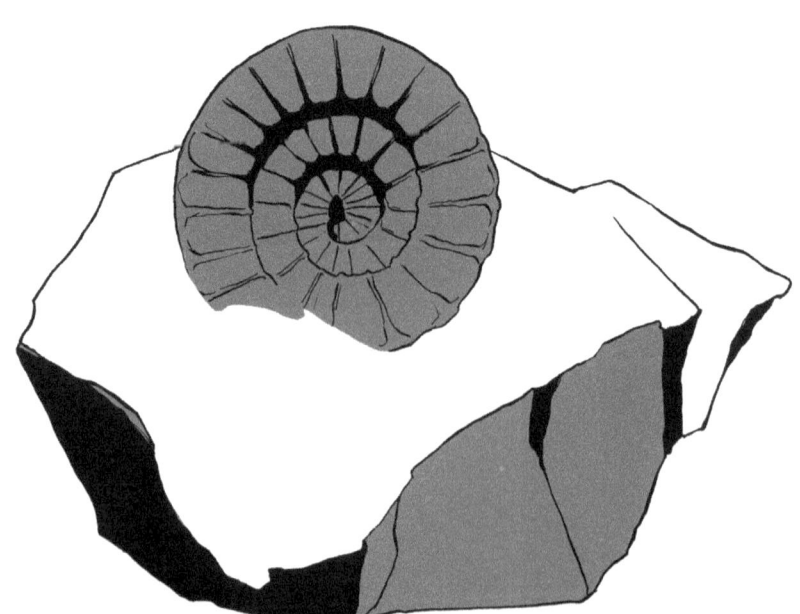

Fish, Bigotry and Self-defense
or The Alien Reconsiders Earth Hobbies

Fishing up a southern mountain, where snow still sits
mid-June. Others line the shore—line upon line

upon line—a string of poles trying to locate
        life. Fish were caught, some swallowed straight
out of the lake into the alien's mouth.

Some caught and let go—She just can't
        get a taste for it. And now the sun arcs low

setting against reflection, as She and the alien paddle
to shore. Packing the tackle and a few uneaten,
unreleased fish

into the trunk, most other day-fishers have already
        fled. One truck a few feet away also loads up.

Caught in mid-motion and the fallen day, a flashlight
        flashes in the alien's face. "Well,
what do we have here?"

Though the question isn't questioning,
just slightly slurred. "I know
what you are," the human man continues, as though

the fact could be hidden. The alien doesn't say a word,
just stares into the bright, lets go

        of his pole and tries to walk, slip
into She's car.
        But, of course, the man is looking for this—looking

for a fight. He blocks the path, storms the new night,
        forcing the alien to assess

humans' violent tendencies, a fragile balance
of tissues.

The Monster Reveals the Grave Robber's Fate

Salt Lake City Cemetery burglar caught in 1862 when Moroni Clawson's naked
corpse was discovered by his brother.

History seems unsure
                        what happened
to the man who dug and robbed
                                at least 300 graves.

Taken into custody and punished with a tattoo
                                         branding him
corrupt, as lynch mobs gathered
                          at the jail.

Unsafe in captivity, unable to swim
                                  authorities brought Jean Baptiste
to one of the lake's islands
                    surrounded by deeper water
and me.

A few weeks of helping himself
                              to ranchers'
cattle for beef, feasting
                  on open air
                            and onions.

And then the dismantling
                    of his shelter,
plank by plank,
            slaughtered cow skinned, tanned

planks lashed together
                to float away
to freedom. The raft's shadow
                        bobbed above

my setting sun
               blocked. Strips of hide pulled apart
opened the raft
         like a handheld paper
                       fan.

Scrambling back
         his back
               at the edge with nowhere
to go, he holds on
         to one wood slab, a dangle

legs adrift
      the unclaimed criminal
facedown
      floated before me, my
eyes, mouth, broken

ears
   I touch to reach
               tattooed
                       forehead and skim his sun

burnt skin
      peeled ink:
             For Robbing the Dead

Four

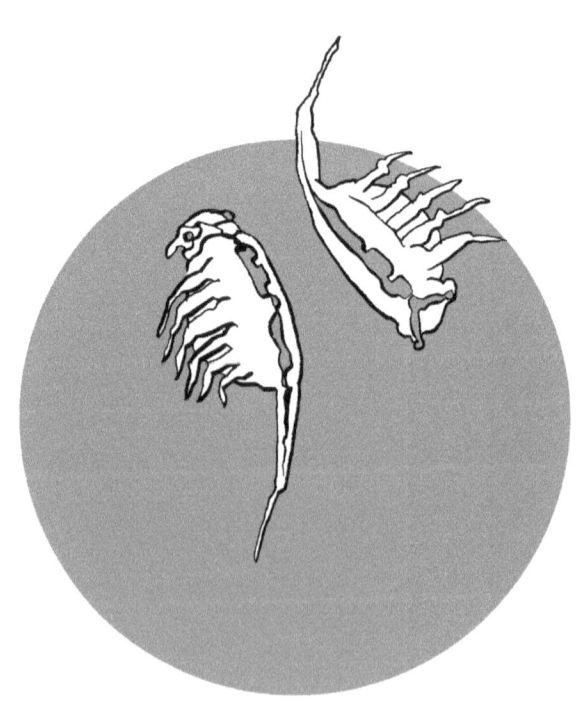

I'm so sorry for the ghost I made you be. Only one of us was real and that was me.

—from "The Treaty," Leonard Cohen

And I brought you into a plentiful country, to eat the fruit thereof and the goodness thereof; but when ye entered, ye defiled my land, and made mine heritage an abomination.

Jeremiah 2:7

The Smog that Rides the Salt Lake/Davis County Line

Out it comes,
equinox-crossed
and it's winter again. She holds her breath.

The aliens haven't adjusted well. They carry inhalers,
wear masks. State-issued
warnings: Avoid

driving, stay inside. None of this air is translucent. It turns
and it turns out this city's in a rut, rated 9th
overall. #9 Toxic.

She licks her lips, a bit
Fire Engine Rose, a hint copper. A peach pit on the counter—
the fruit already in her stomach—

ground up, or bit down

that small core of cyanide
can kill
a bird, a dog, a child. Some aliens

lobby congress for stricter policies: to lessen
the scent of old eggs and black toast. The people shake
hands, nod and grit

statements about basic chemistry, differences in atmosphere.
No burning, fire-
works okay with USE CAUTION. If breathing

is troubled, take heed.

The Great Salt Lake—An Incomplete Timeline, Part VII: Demolished Fences, Cars and Trees

1942:   30 feet high, 100 feet across, an iceberg
        floated from the north. Kept afloat

        long enough to become a winter wonder, a bit
        of a pleasure barge.

1984:   During a period of unusual cold and low salinity,
        a number of large icebergs formed

        roved across the lake, smashing,
        bowling over anything in their way.

Victim:

> *Albatross chick: six months. Cause of death: starvation due to a full stomach. Contents of stomach: cigarette lighters, pump-top sprayer, nut shells, shot gun shell, broken clothespins, hundreds of bits of plastic.*
> —National Geographic picture caption

Cold knots melt in watery bundles;
She takes comfort in the small
pools and chilled air

leaning against chin and wrists.
Flakes of snow string
to the ground, weave and fluff

the city's dressing gown.
She doesn't turn to the alien,
instead sighs straight ahead into frozen

stitches drifting in the street-light glow.
We won't catch these in our mouths,
too dirty... A hand waves at the air,

swats a flake. She thinks of snowballs eaten
from the ground, a child's cold teeth,
a full belly.

Discussing Customs

Alien pokes the dog
in the eye.

The dog flinches.

Alien is
sorry. So sorry.

The dog stares,

Sorry?
You could blind
me.

The dog isn't even
squinting

or actually saying
a word.

A lesson:

This planet requires more
than apologies.

The Trouble with Clothing

What this life wants is a straight line. Speed
of light. To see
what's on the other side of the barrier, the best
way to figure green.

The alien bends, whispers
a curse. He's worn clothing long enough to know
when a seam pops the sound
of a human joint

it means unraveling
a coming ugliness.

But what's undone is done. He lights a match
for comfort

> *a flare, a click*
> *fingertip danger*
> *the sound of wind*
> *months with no rain*
> *burn a field*
> *a burger*
> *books*
> *one water dropped, comes to a hiss*
> *a toilet bowl*
> *heavy traffic on fast forward*
> *strand of smoke*
> *to ceiling*
> *to hose to sky*
> *tobacco*
> *destruction*
> *a snack*

One quick stroke. Like spreading
butter or breaking a string.

Via friction and gravity, a black hole is marked not by absence, but by its interaction with what surrounds it.

Matter that falls on
a black hole can form some of
the brightest objects

in the universe.
Nothing escapes, not even
particles, not light.

The monster looks into the dark heavens and considers how things would be different if he believed in a higher power.

for Derek Haney, in memoriam

Pieces of the past in the blue-black sky,
stars long burnt out, their light just now
reaching Earth's eyes.

He looks up to catch sight
of something that still exists and existed
through his timeline of centuries.

The air is full with changing
seasons. Poking his periphery—
a satellite, a plane, a slab of the moon—

night will not leave
him alone. He searches for a specific
single star

the sign
who cannot show itself tonight.

Jealousy and Greed Are Green or
The Alien Tries to Explain his Flat Temper

Each particle sets the next
in motion, a giant ripple—the universe and its parts
an ocean.

His arms outstretch, fingers spread
the air, as though slowly treading water. *You feel space*
passing, even

when you don't see. Atoms
giving and getting. Everything trying to be
equal, to make a constant.

He stands there looking
ethereal and like a Tai chi instructor.

Me to you
you to something else,
matter is meant to keep moving.

The Great Salt Lake—An Incomplete Timeline, Part VI: Disappearances

1939:   Man claims he lost six horses
           who wandered off
           the natural sandbar into liquid
           sand and sunk.

           Experts know no evidence
           to support the existence
           of underwater quicksand.

The Monster Sees Calves and Feet Off the North Shore

The water is a pink gradient
of pigmented microbes, not clear. Still
his adjusted eyes can view her bare
legs up to the knees

immersed in the lake
She's searching again
the binoculars scanning
for large movement, ripples

without definite origin. As She tries to focus
on the landscape's parts, he hears her
talking to herself
Come on...

Come. On.
Just one piece, one
proof, so I know
I'm more than this

foolish mission. A small sob,
a few extra drops of salt
into the lake. *Show me, monster, show*
show yourself.

If it wasn't certain
exposure, if he wasn't
so enormous, he would swim up
right off shore

to where She wades and touch
each toe lightly. Enough
to make her kick, enough
to give him cause.

The Alien Chose He, but Now Wants to Be a She

        He likes lace—the way skin shows through
        no matter the color—a kind of unnatural
        camo.

The permanent She, the human She
is inconsolable.

        The alien asks questions to puzzle piece the grief.

Her face is a storm
cloud and She can't formulate.

        It's no secret. No matter the pronoun, he is neither
        a he nor a she.

Her mind on spin cycle:
*I wanted androgyny—male androgyny. This house doesn't need
another woman.*

        The alien doesn't understand her despair.
        It's only a costume
        swap, a different role to play.

        Normally tears fascinate
        but there are so many her lids start to swell.

She's always been attracted to the aliens, tall and lean
and open.

This one became more
than a fling, when he showed up in a suit and tie
to her grandfather's funeral.

After hours in separate rooms and thought, a try
at explanation:

You know, I was content being a He, until I lived with your She.

I understand your reasons. Sometimes I wish I was a man. Sometimes neither is enough. But what about you and me?   And what about me?

The Elusive Equation's Solution

The two come together (*satisfied +
happy*) with the whack,

metal bat smacking a piñata.
Bright candy and plastic whistles explode
into the neighbor's yard. She climbs
the chain-link fence,
balances

one leg on each side. Her chest beats
too quick, knowing
the neighbor looks mean, his window
still lit—a sliver of synthetic light
reaches just beyond

her toes. This will be the last time
She attacks a beast of cardboard or flesh

near a property line. This would be
the start
of a bigger hunt for the elusive
solution. (A rainbow simmered
into a well-salted soup.) Before and after, She tries

to sit and only succeeds during the last,
muted sun of day, when the unmoving feels
like moving
forward—the pain of being still
on hold.

A gold wake hits the right side, a hand of setting
rests on her cheek,

bare shoulder. (It's all too beautiful /
to be happy.) Ornate grass fans the breeze,
the perfect model for a bushel of lace.

She grabs what She can
in the dark.

What the Alien Thinks to Say to She

Because human will always feel greater than

Because   brains to species to planets
       indefinite cause with infinite effects

Grandparents, parents with habits   neither of us
can get used to   change

we can't   stop in the middle

There are mollusks and there are bees
               polar bears and elephants

a fight for missing parts

Because we're small and this
has gone
            long

And even if
we're both left-handed   one of us
               has five fingers

Sometimes two things make a maybe, sometimes
an ellipsis   is the story

Because, because

watery lines don't understand
state borders

Tantrum

An orange chucked against the house
drips down the brick
Pebbles sprayed

with aftermath, wipe
their eyes, whisper *careless*

Branches catch one
thought over and over, cradle
let it drop, and won't repeat

The trees, the stones, the brick—
misinterpret

Mostly the thought is periwinkle and hurts.
The orange broken, but still

flavored   She would lick the brick
but should be going
Was leaving when the sound

of catching was destination
enough, and She can't pretend to care
about intent, only effect

or affect   She steps up, samples the brick
fakes good taste   Pebbles

pretend offense   Again
No matter   The branches

will never notice   It's hard to say
what shouldn't have been said

She Writes Notes to the Pagoda Tree, Ties Them to the Branches One by One

I.
Each autumn your petite leaves
surprise with their smart yellow,
a reminder of banana skins, not one
shade different.

II.
I apologize for the way the dog gouged
your thick bark, wanted to climb and grab
the neighbor's cat from your arms. I apologize
for stapling chicken wire around your trunk;
it was meant to stop the clawing. Now I don't know
which was worse.

III.
You are not the Maple. A vast and barrel-chested
guard, a warning, he sloughs his enormous trunk
in large hunks; the wind grunts
lunging through his limbs. You are a cousin
to the pea and your leaves aren't nearly as small
as they seem.

IV.
When I move on from this mountain valley
of hard earth with plenty of snow but little water,
you will be missed. You, who shouldn't
be able to grow here. The arborist says
you're a thirsty breed.

V.
The ground is burning and you must be cold.
This afternoon you released a full yellow
blanket from your branches—not delicate
like a baby—wide and complete.

VI.
How do you gather the courage to let it all go
in a single day?

Here Is What's Left of Lake Bonneville

She is determined to see. Lock the creature in a still, share
his looks with those who'll listen. She takes
a handful of diced tuna. Dabs the juice
from the tin can on her collar bone. The lake is saltier

than the sea, a pH between toothpaste and milk
of magnesia. Salt can't be destroyed—won't dissipate
or burn—all that can be done is grind
the small crystals into dirt and watch it lose

worth. This lesson She learned in Sunday school, the spiritual point
less poignant. Even salt will sift its way
to shore, the edges of his liquid home. One toe
at a time, She dribbles fish purée,

until She is up to her earlobes. Empty
cans bob near outstretched fists. Mosquitoes line her forehead.
Torso stripped, eyes closed. A lake
housing a monster with nowhere else to go,

without a single outlet, it's up to the earth's inventions now.

Notes and Sources

"Great Salt Lake Timeline"

Poem partially found in:
- http://www.deseretnews.com/article/710391/Great-tales-sur rounding-the-Great-Salt-Lake.html
- http://mysteriousuniverse.org/2015/02/the-great-mysteries-of-the-great-salt-lake/
- https://en.wikipedia.org/wiki/North_Shore_Monster
  https://en.wikipedia.org/wiki/Antelope_Island_bison_herd

"Munchie Sightings…"

- *The Great Salt Lake* by Dale L. Morgan, Scribner, 1995; originally Bobbs-Merrill Company, 1947.

"The Alien Takes the Human's Tears"

After "Topography of Tears" a photo series by Rose-Lynn Fisher and "The Microscopic Structures of Dried Human Tears" by Joseph Stromberg, *Smithsonianmag.com*: http://www.smithsonianmag.com/science-nature/the-microscopic-structures-of-dried-human-tears-180947766/

"Utah Complications"

The Mormons reached the American West in 1847 and settled in Utah following violent conflicts and religious discrimination in Illinois and Missouri (partially due to their practicing polygamy). The "Miracle of the Gulls" occurred in 1848, when a flock of seagulls flew into the Salt Lake Valley and ate hoards of insects that were demolishing the crops, thus saving the Mormons from starvation. In 1857 at Mountain Meadows in southern Utah, the Baker-Fancher emigrant wagon train was attacked by a militia of Mormon settlers; 120–140 people were killed, mostly families on their way to California. The US Army attacked a Shoshone camp at the Bear River in 1863, after years of clashes and raids on farms in northern Utah—at least 240 Shoshone were killed.

- Harold B. Lee Library: "Seagulls, Miracle of" by Richard W. Sadler: http://eom.byu.edu/index.php/Seagulls,_Miracle_of
- *Pioneer.Utah.gov*: Utah State Bird–Sea Gull: http://onlinelibrary.utah.gov/research/utah_symbols/bird.html
- *MRM.org*, "Was There a 'Miracle' of the Seagulls?" by Bill McKeever: http://www.mrm.org/seagulls

"The Monster Reveals the Grave Robber's Fate"

- *Deseret News*: "Great Tales Surrounding the Great Salt Lake...": http://www.deseretnews.com/article/710391/Great-tales-surrounding-the-Great-Salt-Lake.html
- *The Salt Lake Tribune*: "Wharton: Grave Robber Finds redemption on Antelope Island." : http://archive.sltrib.com/story.php?ref=/sltrib/neighborhooddaviscounty/53888739-123/baptiste-grave-island-movie.html.csp#&ui-state=dialog
- *Historytogo.utah.gov*: "Unsolved Mysteries in Utah—The Bizarre Case of Grave Robber Jean Baptiste": http://historytogo.utah.gov/utah_chapters/pioneers_and_cowboys/thecaseofgraverobberjean-baptiste.html

"The Monster Looks Into the Dark…"

The lines "night will not leave / him alone" are borrowed and adapted from Sean Rowe's song, "I Can't Make a Living From Holding You."

General Sources

- *Brigham Young: Pioneer Prophet* by John G. Turner, Belknap Press: An Imprint of Harvard University Press, 2014
- *American Crucifixion: The Murder of Joseph Smith and the Fate of the Mormon Church* by Alex Beam, PublicAffairs, 2014
- *Visions of Antelope Island and Great Salt Lake* by Marlin Stum, Utah State University Press, 1999
- http://www.historytogo.utah.gov/
- https://en.wikipedia.org/wiki/Great_Salt_Lake
- https://en.wikipedia.org/wiki/Water

Acknowledgments

Extended gratitude to the slew of people who helped create this strange creature of a book, whether through feedback or friendship. Special thanks to:

- Chris Smith, the man who is Quarter Press, who made this whole thing more beautiful than imagined.
- Maximiliane Spieß whose illustrations make these pages special.
- My family who supports me and my ideas, when they understand and when they do not.
- My love, my favorite, my Nano—for believing in me, my writing, and this book much longer than I could.
- My teachers at Utah State University and Lesley University, specifically Brock Dethier, Star Coulbrooke, Paul Crumbly, Robert Winward, Teresa Cader, Spencer Reece, Thomas Sayers Ellis, Janet Sylvester, and Steven Cramer.
- My cohorts, writing groups, and others who provided critique, inspiration, and encouragement to write about aliens and monsters. A shout to Danielle Beazer Dubrasky, Jerry VanIeperen, John Kippen, Shari Zollinger, Adrianna Jorgensen-Bryan, Wendy Blackenship, Michael McLane, Matthew Bennett, Sandy Anderson, Shanan Ballam, Yolanda Franklin, Robin Linn, Lauren Norton, Karin Davidson, Todd Robinson, Liz Kay, Jen Lambert, Lisa Bickmore, and Katie Bradley Barrett.

And a last thanks to all of the editors and publications that first gave these poems a place in the world:

- *15 Bytes*: "Capitol Reef"
- *A Capella Zoo*: "Tantrum"
- *burntdistrict*: "A Floridian Says, 'I Could Never Live in a Place Like That.'"
- *Blossom as the Cliffrose: Mormon Legacies and the Beckoning Wild Anthology*, Torrey House Press, 2021: "Darwin Applied with a Garden Hose" and "Utah Complications"
- *Blue Earth Review*: "The Monster Sees Calves and Feet off the North Shore," "The Monster Reveals the Grave Robber's Fate"
- *Cherry Tree*: "Fox Mulder and the Vampire Slayer"
- *Dark Mountain*: "Utah Complications"

- *Drunken Boat*: "The Mums Are Always Dying"
- *Emrys Journal*: "Discussing Customs"
- *Consecrate/Desecrate: Great Salt Lake Anthology*, Great Salt Lake Collaborative, 2022: "The lake monster looks into the dark heavens and considers how things would be different if he believed in a higher power.," "An Ambush of Major and Minor—the Monster Sings," "The Great Salt Lake has been shrinking since the rounding of the last ice age," "The Monster Reveals the Grave Robber's Fate," "Here Is What's Left of Lake Bonneville"
- *Green Mountains Review*: "The Smog that Rides the Salt Lake/Davis County Line"
- *The Midwest Quarterly*: "HonK's $1 Store"
- *Origins Journal*: "What the Alien Thinks to Say to She," "Sunday Dinners Are Awkward"
- *Open: A Journal of Arts & Letters*: "The Alien Takes the Human's Tears," "Exhausted by more than just tears and empty ice cube trays, the human addresses the alien's water experiments.," "Much of the Universe's," "Jealousy and Greed Are Green or The Alien Tries to Explain his Flat Temper," "Victim:," "71% of the Earth's Surface"
- *Pamplemousse*: "Here Is What's Left of Lake Bonneville," "The Alien Chose He, but Now Wants to Be a She"
- *Pilgrimage*: "The Great Salt Lake has been shrinking since the rounding of the last ice age." "Monster Stalks Seagulls," "The Flamingo on Shore—Pink Floyd, an Aviary Escapee"
- *Psaltery & Lyre*: "This Rainbow"
- *The Quarter(ly)*: "Fish, Bigotry and Self-defense or The Alien Reconsiders Earth Hobbies," "The Alien Collects a Pet," "Alien Discovers a Sweet Tooth"
- *South Dakota Review*: "Too Many Humans End in a Crash," "Alien and She Visit the North," "The Trouble with Clothing," "'Kelpie' Sounds Nicer than 'Monster,'" "The Monster Laughs at the Accounts," "Of Course the Monster Had a Mother"
- *Rattle*: "Discussing Earth's Insects"
- *Rock & Sling*: "Attempt #2 to Spot the Monster," "What She Misses About Being Mormon," "An Ambush of Major and Minor—the Monster Sings," "Pretending to be interviewed, the monster gets choked up, tells the cameraman to shut the damn thing off."
- *saltfront*: "For Classification Purposes"
- *Spillway*: "Sorting Bulk"

- *Superstition Review*: "Notes on Earth Life"
- *Terrain.org*: "Great White Sharks Must Move Forward to Breathe"
- *The Shore*: "Earth Ghosts," "Stuck in a Watery Still"
- *Tidal Basin Review*: "She Writes Notes to the Pagoda Tree, Ties Them to the Branches One by One"
- *The Wax Paper*: "Sacrament Started the Three Hours of Church on Sunday"

The manuscript was a finalist for Letras Latinas' Andrés Montoya Poetry Prize, Word Work's Hilary Tham Capital Collection prize, and Inlandia Institute's Hillary Gravendyk Prize, as well as long listed for the The Brittingham & Felix Pollak Prizes and YesYes Book's open reading period.

Maxi Spieß, born in 1992, has studied illustration, once upon a time mainly focussing on comics, and creative writing. She lives in a rather catholic city in western Germany, where she works as an illustrator and is writing novels in her free time. Her favourite techniques include ink drawing and lino cut, everything that provides stark black-and-white contrasts; her creativity is fuelled by coffee, bagpipes, and spiraling trips down research-rabbitholes.

Natalie Padilla Young co-founded and manages the poetry magazine *Sugar House Review*. By day, she works as an art director for a Salt Lake City ad agency. Her poetry has appeared in *Green Mountains Review*, *Tampa Review*, *Rattle*, *South Dakota Review*, *Los Angeles Times*, *Tar River Poetry*, *Terrain.org*, and others. Natalie grew up Mormon in Utah with a Puerto Rican mom and a dad who is a "direct descendent" of Brigham Young.

Natalie serves on the boards of Utah Arts and Lightscatter Press. She lives in southern Utah with the poet Nano Taggart and two dogs. Find more at *NatalieYoungArts.com* or follow her on Instagram, *@pickledbeatss*, for many pup pics.

www.ingramcontent.com/pod-product-compliance
Lightning Source LLC
Chambersburg PA
CBHW040251090526
44586CB00041B/2781